IN THE ORIENTAL STYLE

MICHAEL FREEMAN
SIÂN EVANS
MIMI LIPTON

IN THE

A Bulfinch Press Book

Little, Brown and Company

Boston New York Toronto London

ORIENTAL STYLE

A Sourcebook of Decoration and Design

Page 1 Carved wooden bargeboard from Ban Tab Salak, Thailand.
Title page Korean medicine chest with Thai hill-tribe basketwork.
Pages 6 and 7 A teashop in Liverpool in thoroughly traditional
Japanese style; the visual emphasis is upon the use of natural
materials and simple rectilinear forms to promote a
sense of harmony and tranquility.

First North American Paperback Edition

ISBN 0–8212-2367–4
Library of Congress Catalog Card Number 90–55397

Bulfinch Press is an imprint and trademark of
Little, Brown and Company (Inc.)
Published simultaneously in Canada by
Little, Brown & Company (Canada) Limited

PRINTED IN SINGAPORE

Contents

PREFACE

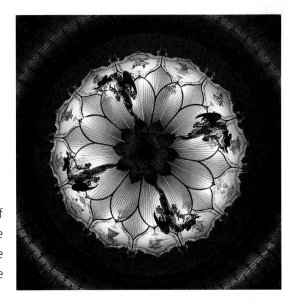

From the beginnings of global trade, the West has looked to the Orient as a fertile source of beautiful objects and exotic materials. Occidental architects, artists and designers have constantly used the East as a nursery of ideas in style and construction. This tradition of exchange has intensified as the cultures of south-east Asia have become more immediately accessible to the West through increased travel opportunities and the rapid economic growth of the region.

This book identifies what constitutes 'Oriental' style, both traditional and contemporary, in settings as diverse as the city of Tokyo, the villages of Thailand and apartments in New York, London and Paris. Perhaps it should be emphasized now that there is no single, definitive 'Oriental' style, but rather a wealth of diverse treatments and approaches. The numerous examples illustrated on the pages which follow range from authentic traditional interiors to the exuberant, eclectic blending of arts and artifacts from a variety of sources in recreations of Oriental styles in the West.

In our examples of Oriental design and decoration we can discern three broad categories. The first consists of the straightforward recreation of traditional homes and gardens. The second is the late twentieth-century version of the enthusiastic response of many nineteenth-century decorators and their clients who used the forms, motifs and colour schemes of the Far East to create an ambience of exoticism in Western settings, often basing their schemes on secondary sources, such as photographs and illustrations. The results were sometimes bizarre, but no one could deny the strong visual impact of the imported motifs and whole settings. Examples range from the ubiquitous 'sunrise' design found in domestic and civic architecture throughout Europe and America in the nineteen-twenties and thirties to the exteriors of 'Chinese-style' picture palaces and Asian restaurants.

A third category, superficially the least overtly 'Oriental' in character, is the result of the search by Modern Movement architects and designers for solutions to the pressing Western problem of overcrowded cities. In creating simple and flexible domestic environments many architects (most notably, Frank Lloyd Wright) adopted devices from Far Eastern interior design: modules, low-level stacking or folding furniture, built-in storage units and curtain walling or screens to create environments which are aesthetically pleasing yet functional and versatile.

As the East becomes closer and more accessible to the average Westerner the more we may expect to see its cultural diversity, decorative forms, vibrant colours, its arts, crafts and artifacts underline the unique appeal of Oriental style. The following pages are a celebration of this process.

An early nineteenth-century blend of 'Chinese' style crossed with a rococo interpretation of Indian styles, this chinoiserie interior was originally installed in the Brighton Pavilion, but was later removed to Buckingham Palace **(opposite)**. An ornate central light fitting in the Brighton Pavilion features that perennial motif of the Far East, the mythical dragon **(above)**. The inspiration for many 'Orientalist' decorative interiors was taken from designs on imported blue and white Chinese ceramics, such as this cobalt Kangxi jar decorated with insects, flowering plants and stylized rock formations **(below)**.

Far Eastern artists realistically portrayed their experience of the burgeoning ports as Oriental trade expanded during the nineteenth century, providing factual records of the growth of major cities; a Chinese export painting of Canton graphically depicts the activity in the American and French concessions **(left above)**, and despite the obvious difference in styles, recalls the almost 'documentary' approach of an earlier Chinese pictorial rug showing the grounds of the Summer Palace **(left below)**. However, romantic visions of the perceived grace, charm and elegance of Oriental life inflamed the creative imaginations of Western artists and designers, because such idyllic images contrasted so strongly with the effects of mass industrialization in their own cultures. A. H. Schramm's *Decorating Buddha's Shrine* **(opposite above left)** and Eliza Turck's *The Doll's Tea Party* **(opposite below)** reveal the fascination which the Orient held for European painters of the nineteenth century. This fascination was extensively transferred into the world of commerce in the Edwardian era, as this commemorative postcard from the Japan-British Exhibition of 1910 testifies **(opposite above right)**.

Spring, Japan-British Exhibition, London 1910

THE LOOK OF THE ORIENT

The contemporary Orient is a heady and sometimes disconcerting blend of old and new; the essential pragmatism of its peoples has led to the adoption of certain aspects of Western living, but not at the expense of far older, deeper cultural ideals and customs. The ancient, expressed in the stairway of a Japanese shrine **(opposite)**, for instance, is revered out of a deep-seated sense of respect for one's ancestors, and new ways of living are grafted on to time-honoured customs. Although there are many 'looks' of the Orient – there can be few greater contrasts than that between cosmopolitan Hong Kong and Lhasa, the remote capital of Tibet – there is still a certain homogeneity of approach to style and design among the peoples of eastern Asia, mainly due to the all-pervasive influence of China. This manifests itself in respect for underlying harmony and order, derived from Confucianism, Buddhism and the way of life known as Tao. The latter is also characterized by complex symbolism expressing the balancing forces (*yin* and *yang*) of the universe, which is taken up in many of the traditional practical and decorative arts in areas which have come under the influence of Chinese culture.

The quintessential look of the Orient is achieved by close attention to detail and the constant renewal of traditional craft processes. Examples range from the riotously colourful carved wooden masks of Indonesia **(opposite left)** and the brilliantly hued waxed paper and bamboo parasols of Chiangmai **(opposite right)** to the sympathetic and delicate presentation of food **(above)**. The careful selection of a Japanese fan-shaped dish or Burmese lacquerware to complement the colour and texture of the meal is an indication of the respect paid to the guest and reveals an acute awareness of the desired visual impact. Similarly, meticulous attention to detail is evident in the intricate costume and gestures of the classical Javanese dancer **(below right)**, the restrained opulence of a tiny Fabergé Buddha **(right)**, and the careful wrapping of young trees in a Korean garden **(below)**.

Colour and attention to detail abound in all aspects of Oriental life, and are particularly associated with the homes of the wealthy and the decoration of religious structures: Puri Saren Palace, Bali **(opposite)**; the *naga* roof finial of Thailand **(above)**, and the façade of Wat San Pakoi Temple, northern Thailand, at sunset **(right)**.

The ornately decorative use of precious metals in glowing colours is widespread in much of Oriental architecture. In contrast to Western values, the lavish ornamentation of the exterior of a building in the East commands respect for the institution and the individuals responsible for it, rather than envy or derision at such ostentation. In Thailand, especially, the practice of donating money to enable the further decoration and refurbishment of the local Buddhist temple is still considered a meritorious act. Consequently, the state of a temple is often a more accurate indicator of local prosperity than the seemingly humble dwellings grouped around it.

The combination of gold or gilt with brilliantly-coloured enamels or inlaid stones is particularly prevalent in Burma and Thailand; certain examples, such as the Wat Rajabopit in Bangkok **(opposite)**, also reveal a profound influence from India. The gilded, relief-moulded peacock of Wat Pan Thao **(above left)** guards the doorway to the *viharn* or assembly hall, and a carved wooden window frame in the same complex is ornamented with gold inlaid with mica fragments **(below right)**. A detail from the golden *chedi* of Wat Haripunchai in northern Thailand **(above right)** forms a fascinating sequence of undulating columns, while a jade boulder **(below left)** from the Jewellery Hall of the Forbidden City reveals an exquisitely worked, stylized, classical Chinese landscape.

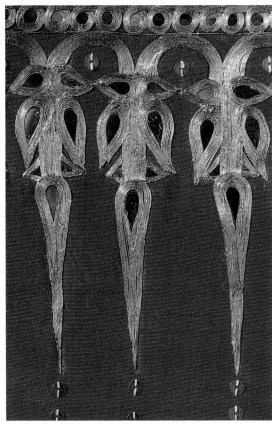

Colourful naturalistic motifs abound in Oriental arts and crafts, reflecting the interdependence of man and the environment. Brilliantly-hued patterns of stylized plants and flowers adorn windows in a South Korean temple **(right above)**, and also feature in Indonesian glass **(right below)**. Colour and pattern derived from the natural world recur in a multiplicity of artefacts from the Orient: a painted panel from Korea **(opposite above left)**; the exquisite fruit and vegetable carving of Thailand **(opposite below left)**; puppets from Indonesia **(opposite above right)**; silk from Chiangmai **(opposite below right)**.

The plethora of traditional forms, motifs and finishes displayed in the window of a ceramics shop in Seoul **(left)** betrays a variety of indigenous and foreign styles, but paramount throughout the region is the all-pervasive influence of pre-revolutionary China, which can be seen as the cultural motherlode of the Far East, a power expressed in the Meridian Gate **(opposite)** of the Forbidden City, Beijing (detail).

The *naga* or mythical water serpent of Thailand is the favoured form of roof finials for temples **(left)**, so that the structure may be protected against evil spirits bent on destroying the building; however, the aid of benevolent forces is also enlisted, as in the offerings to promote fertility made at a Buddhist temple in Kamakura, Japan **(below)**.

Display and presentation of even the most humble market vegetables is an integral factor in determining the look of the Orient; sake barrels, calligraphy brushes and ceramics are stacked deep but with a view to displaying them at their best **(left and below)**, a format successfully adopted by both a London retail store **(bottom left)** and a Bangkok antiques emporium **(right)**.

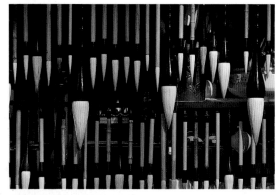

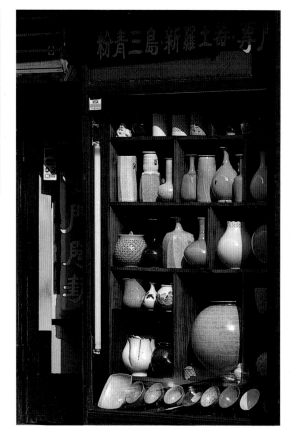

TRADITIONAL LIVING

The construction and forms of traditional Oriental domestic buildings are, naturally, a response to local and climatic conditions and availability of materials. They are also, in their variations of style, expressions of the deeper preoccupations and aspirations of each culture; in short, they are the physical manifestation of fundamental philosophies, religions and cultural beliefs. The tree under which the Buddha found 'enlightenment', for instance, may be seen reflected in the wooden pillar-and-beam construction on a solid base **(opposite)**, overhung by substantial eaves, of much Oriental building, although this varies according to specific climatic and geographical circumstances.

One dominant characteristic of traditional Oriental housing is the sense of flexibility and of available space in the interior. Rooms are often decorated in unadorned natural materials and are largely unfurnished, allowing the use of the space for a wide variety of everyday activities. The simplicity, even austerity, of taste derived from Buddhism, means that much of family life is conducted on floor mats or cushions, or on the verandah if the climate permits. Furniture is generally kept to a minimum and can be stacked or stored when not in use. Interiors are often subdivided by sliding doors or walls; in warmer climates, latticework or carved wooden transom panels immediately below ceiling level allow the free circulation of air. In Korean and Japanese settings, notably, translucent hand-made rag or rice paper is pasted across interior windows and partitions, allowing a subtle diffusion of light.

The spreading eaves, soaring gables and low-pitched roofs of rural South Korean homes betray a major stylistic influence from China. Yet in their pillar-and-beam construction, their overhanging roofs and curtain-walling, they are also physical manifestations of the Buddhist belief that this existence is merely transitory, and that the home should therefore be considered as a temporary shelter, a physical base from which to seek spiritual enlightenment. The Buddha gained enlightenment while resting under a tree, and the 'parasol' structure of much traditional domestic building throughout the region can be likened to the shelter provided by groves of trees, which can provide a refuge from the stresses, strains and storms of everyday life. The metaphor is heightened by the overt use of unadorned timber and barely-finished tree trunks to make up the visible skeleton of the building.

In the hotter, more humid countries, traditional buildings enable the inhabitants to withstand the climate by providing what is effectively a series of interconnected roofs supported by pillars and subdivided by curtain walls. The various components of the home are linked by covered walkways, as in the Kamtheing House, Bangkok **(opposite)**. Trees and vegetation grow between the split-level terraces, and the blurring of boundaries between the house and the landscape is also apparent in the variety of undecorated natural woods used as building materials. A simple teak door-latch **(below right)** has an intrinsic sculptural appeal, while the weathered exterior of a temple meeting-house **(above left and above right, below left)** is a testament both to the pride of local carpenters and the vicissitudes of the climate.

The layout of Thai buildings generally consists of a sequence of structures, linked by verandahs and covered walkways. The verandahs of this ancient house in Bangkok allow access between the rooms without infringing on the inhabitants' privacy **(left above and left below)**. Carved wooden panelling **(opposite)** and slatted windows create an air of ordered simplicity, and are a testament to the skills of the craftsmen who constructed the house.

In traditional Oriental rural dwellings, the kitchen is one of the few rooms with a specific, clearly-defined function; furthermore, it often provides the focal point for the informal activities of the household.

As in the rest of the house, there is little in the way of furniture or fittings in the Western sense; most food preparation and cooking is done while squatting on mats on the floor, and so the cooking ranges are at a suitably low level. In Korean farmers' kitchens **(opposite above and below left)** small serving tables which act as individual trays for meals are stacked on one side when not needed, while handwoven baskets of assorted sizes are piled up on a shelf at eyelevel; decorative *sake* containers are stored on a chest **(opposite below right)**. Similarly, in a traditional Thai kitchen **(right)**, unnecessary utensils are slung overhead in a suspended rack, although those implements in constant use remain within easy reach. Dry goods, cooking oils and perishable foodstuffs must be kept safe from marauding insects and animals, so they are stored in large ceramic jars with tight-fitting lids.

Adequate ventilation in the kitchen is essential, especially in those parts of the Far East where the weather becomes very hot and humid during the summer. It is therefore common in houses of this kind to find the windows unglazed and unscreened; the Thai kitchen is located at the corner of the structure so that two windows set at right angles to each other maximize the effects of any passing breezes.

Sleeping arrangements vary throughout the region depending upon the climate and local customs; in this traditional rural house outside Bangkok **(left)**, the 'bedroom' as Westerners understand the term does not exist. The sleeping area is designated by the provision of simple flat mattresses which fold up when not required, and curtains give some privacy. Ventilation comes through the unglazed window, which also has wooden shutters, and a large mosquito net protects the inhabitants from that local scourge.

This house in Chiangmai contains a low Thai bedstead in teak. The carved wooden pediment forming the bedhead is an example of architectural salvage, and the design is typical of the 'flame' configuration found on much of the traditional architecture of Thailand. The outline of the carving suits the high-pitched ceiling of the room.

The *tokonoma*, or traditional alcove of Japanese architecture, provides a focal point for aesthetic expression in the interior **(above)**. Objects for contemplation, such as hanging scrolls or *ikebana* flower arrangements are carefully chosen to enhance what might otherwise be a somewhat austere setting. Although not conforming to the time-honoured *tatami* mat module, as found in the traditional house, the *tokonoma* still fulfils an essential rôle in a modern house in Beppu **(opposite)**; here the emphasis upon natural, unadorned materials is even more evident in the choice of bamboo trunks as the *higashi-daira*, or main pillar, of the recess.

A quintessentially traditional Japanese approach dictated the creation of this tea ceremony complex; in fact, these settings are located in a converted stable block in the centre of Manhattan.

ORIENTAL STYLES EAST AND WEST

Interior decoration in the style of the Far East is a fascinating mélange of motifs and forms: high-tech sophistication sits alongside indigenous imagery and craftsmanship. The International Modernism of the apartment blocks of Hong Kong is paired with the opulence of Chinese moulded ceilings or the rigorous simplicity of the Japanese bath-house. Keeping a foot in both camps is a delicate but rewarding balancing act, as in this Paris interior **(opposite)** which joyfully blends objects from East and West.

The single most profound difference between Oriental and Western approaches to home decoration lies in the definition of different areas within it; the former is neutral, the latter specific. Westerners grow up with the notion that each room has a clearly stated purpose and function; when one is in use, then the others become 'dead space', and architects and designers reflect this in urban environments by dividing already restricted space into even tinier units. In the Orient, virtually every room, with the exceptions of kitchen and bathroom, is considered a 'living room' – and dining room, and bedroom. Much Oriental furniture is designed for its adaptability; modern Chinese, Korean or Japanese furniture for city dwellers is lightweight, while sliding doors as room dividers are invaluable in the confined spaces of city apartments.

Although such overall design considerations have been a very important feature of Far Eastern influence on the West, the most dramatic effects in interior design in the Oriental style are undoubtedly those derived from the rich colouring and intricate detailing of many Eastern artifacts. The small scale and exquisite decorative qualities of lacquerwork, textiles and carvings make them peculiarly suitable for display in limited spaces. Dominant colours of cinnabar red, black and gold can bring an effect of exotic luxury and richness to any interior. Even the heavier pieces of furniture, often made with the export market in mind, usually have a high 'display' value. The interiors illustrated on the following pages will repay careful analysis of the effects achieved through the combination of colour, light and objects, from Japanese screens to Thai tables and Burmese lacquerware.

Hallways introduce the ambience of the interior – they are difficult places to decorate adequately, but should provide a hint of the nature of the rest of the setting. Two contrasting approaches are evident here. A brightly lit, severely minimalist, and rather rugged entrance hall to offices along Japanese modernist lines suggests an efficient, practical environment. The monochrome lattice-textured wallpaper of the hall of a London apartment **(opposite)** provides the perfect backdrop to the sinuous, sensual forms of Chinese rosewood furniture and fine antique ceramics, creating a softer, more intimate mood.

Completely Oriental style buildings
are still comparatively rare in the West, so this
example in Paris is remarkable for its
uncompromising promulgation of traditional
Chinese style. The interior is a sequence of
rooms whose windows are barred with
decorative lattice work **(right above and
below)**, and the wooden furniture is low-
level and features *kang* style – inwardly-curving
– legs. The moon-shaped opening between
one public room and another is a form
commonly found in garden and external wall
construction in pre-revolutionary Chinese
buildings, but here it facilitates movement
between the two spaces. The interior
(opposite) is handsomely panelled in rich,
dark wood; the pierced transoms allow
ventilation while impressing the visitor with
their understated opulence. The exterior of the
building **(opposite lower right)** is roofed
with flying gables in classical Chinese style, and
the approach to the entrance is defined by a
traditional roofed gateway; the encircled
Chinese character signifies long life and
prosperity.

Vibrant Eastern colour schemes can create a unique and personal version of Oriental style in the interiors of Western apartments and houses. The use of lacquered furniture and panelling in traditional shades of cinnabar red and black in these three interiors evokes an attractively warm and inviting atmosphere; it also provides a suitably unifying backdrop or visual counterpoint to the wide variety of Far Eastern art objects displayed. Two Japanese *noh* masks are placed against a Chinese painting **(above left)** and flanked by a Chinese lacquered cabinet. Another view of the same apartment **(below left)** shows the owner's collection of framed Chinese paintings against a custom-made red lacquer wall-panel, a successful stylistic hybrid which combines the traditional colours of China with rectilinear grid motifs derived from Japanese *shoji*. The Chinese table in the foreground is modern, while the gold-coloured blooms are Japanese.

This bedroom (opposite) in a London town house is presided over by a carving of a Chinese sage housed in an alcove above a Japanese trousseau trunk. Although the room is small, the location of an antique wooden carving and a Chinese lacquered panel at this height provides the valuable illusion of space. The overtly Chinese theme is reiterated in the opulent colour scheme and the lustrous sheen of the rich, subdued tones of the decorative lacquer panel, contributing to the ambience of exotic, sensuous luxury.

The decoration of bathrooms presents a wonderful opportunity for the application of Oriental style. High summer temperatures in this Andalusian house **(left)** dictated the use of marble, whose coolness of colour and touch makes it the ideal material. However, the understated classicism of the stone is enlivened by the antique Burmese gable end mounted on the wall, and a carved wooden panel inset on one fascia of the bath surround. The superb sculptural qualities of these pieces provide vital focal points in this otherwise simple, almost minimalist room.

The bathroom of a small London house (opposite) deliberately evokes an atmosphere of seductive luxury; strings of miscellaneous small objects, beads and carvings collected throughout the Far East are suspended over the bath to entertain the eye, and Thai and Burmese lacquered receptacles contain larger pieces of Oriental jewellery. A richly resonant colour scheme further adds to the impression of sensuousness and opulence.

An exquisite and intricate Tibetan devotional picture
(**thanka**) adorns the wall of a bedroom in a large country house, and
handwoven woollen rugs from the Far East cover the floors. The
asymmetrical shapes and fascias of two antique Japanese *tansu* chests
have a quietly resonant charm as well as providing ample storage space
and a broad, low-level surface for the display of favourite objects.

Simple Thai furniture makes an attractive and practical addition to this terrace overlooking a range of hills in southern Spain. The uncomplicated forms of the bamboo day beds and parasol, also from Thailand, look completely at home in a setting of rough stonework and terracotta tiles. The upholstery of the beds is covered in a sturdy *Ikat* material from north-east Thailand. An ornamental palm provides a dramatic centrepiece for the whole arrangement.

Low-level tables are an integral part of Oriental life, and can be successfully used in Western settings as an ideal surface for the display of decorative objects. Examples of such tables can be seen in these three interiors **(right)**, including a particularly fine antique table from Thailand **(above)**, a Japanese table inlaid with mother-of-pearl **(centre)** and one from Indonesia **(below)**. It is interesting to note that in all these interiors, not only are the objects of Far Eastern origin, but they are also arranged in a way which owes a great deal to traditional Oriental practice. In one case, an exquisite gold screen **(opposite)** provides a backdrop to the central focal point of the table, and plants or flower arrangements break up the harder edges of the furniture.

The owner of this New York apartment successfully employed an Oriental approach to the interior design of her home, and the result is a pleasing, harmonious combination of objects and artefacts drawn from a number of Far Eastern countries. The dark colours and rich surfaces of Oriental furniture can appear heavy and oppressive if cluttered and jammed together; in this living room each piece seems to sit comfortably with its neighbours. The antique wooden chest from Tibet in the living room **(opposite)** is painted with exquisite scenes, imbued with the subtle patina of age. The geometric design of the original parquet floor is accentuated by the diagonal pattern of the handwoven Tibetan rug, but the harder lines are alleviated by Chinese touches; the scroll-mounted ancestor painting and the statues soften the angles, while an unusual display of flowers in a Japanese basket breaks the rectilinear theme.

Across the room, a particularly fine Chinese table in yuna wood is flanked by traditional rosewood armchairs **(right above)**, providing a suitable foil for the curved, elegant forms of the Ming horse and statue of Buddha. Similarly, an important piece of statuary is silhouetted against the window **(right below)**; the sinuous lines of the Javanese deer combine with the abstract patterns of the Tibetan tiger rug to provide movement and texture in this well-chosen and unobtrusive Oriental scheme.

In a small London apartment, the challenge of making the most of a limited space has been successfully met by adopting a traditional Japanese approach; an illusion of ample space is created by blending the best of East and West. The work and leisure areas of the living room (**top**) are recessed in the fashion of a *tokonoma* (traditional meditational recess), and the bookshelves are stepped in the manner of *chigai-dana*, or 'broken mist' shelves. Translucent screens allow ample light without distracting the inhabitants, and the floor area is left uncluttered and simple.

Sliding *fusuma* (screens) divide the living room from the bedroom, which is a masterpiece in Japanese-style understatement (**left and opposite below**). Wooden structural elements remain unpainted and unadorned, relying for their visual impact on the beauty of the natural wood grain. The resulting rectilinear scheme is echoed in the geometric pattern of the futon cover. Air and light circulate through the *ramma* or grille between ceiling and room dividers, and built-in closets discreetly conceal the impedimenta of everyday life.

The kitchen of this apartment (above) is the room which is the least overtly Japanese in style, yet it retains many of the essential characteristics of modern Oriental city dwelling. The grid effect of *shoji* over the window is repeated in the rectilinear format of the bank of built-in storage units, while the continuous bench of working surface on the opposite wall allows a small space to be effectively used by the occupants. Lightweight stools tuck under the counter when not required, and the result is a pleasant and efficient working environment.

Both the closet space and *tokonoma* recess (above) conform to the dimensions of *tatami* mats; cupboard doors and *fusuma* interior partitions can be opened to maximize the floor space.

Natural light streams through the *shoji,* the sliding window frames covered in translucent rice paper; the grid motif echoes the geometric scheme so typical of traditional Japanese rooms.

The emphasis upon the exposed pillar and beam construction of the traditional Japanese dwelling **(left)** is particularly apparent in this house in Kyoto, and the interplay of timbers and articulated, interpenetrating space bears more than a passing resemblance to the Mackintosh Library in Glasgow. Carefully selected *tansu* chests and ceramic pieces are highlighted by their considered location in relation to the regular geometric division of the wall surfaces **(opposite)**.

The rich colours and exotic forms of Oriental furniture and objects make an exciting and dramatic display against the neutral background of this living room in a London town house. Particularly striking are the lacquered bowls from Thailand and the hanging textile from Indonesia. The table and the chair on the right are both antique Thai pieces which combine easily with the modern Italian leather sofa.

The combination of modern European and traditional Oriental design is continued in the bedroom of the same house. The minimalist form of an angled 'Tizio' lamp nicely complements the opulence of an Indonesian bed cover, while the simplicity and ingenuity of much Oriental design is present in the form of the Chinese lacquered baskets to the left of the photograph.

Just a few miles north of Rome, this modern Italian house consists of a series of interrelated spaces suggestive of the traditional Oriental dwelling. It is appropriate therefore that most of the decorative objects in the sitting and dining areas **(left and above)** are from Thailand, Cambodia and Laos. This extensive open space on the ground floor is notable for its decorative use of statuary and other objects, creating a lively and uncluttered effect; especially impressive is the cylindrical form of a Thai ceremonial drum.

This English country house has been refurnished using a collection of fascinating and unusual Oriental pieces, particularly from Tibet **(above)**. The serpentine forms of a set of antique Chinese furniture are the spectacular focal points of the living room **(right)**.

The powerful religious iconography and symbolism of the Orient abounds in these two interiors; particularly fine Tibetan *thankas* are displayed on the walls, while the rug features a design incorporating the swastika, an ancient Hindu symbol meaning eternal life, which is also found throughout China, Tibet and Japan.

Behind the façade of this house in the centre of Paris lies a series of interiors furnished almost entirely in the Oriental style. The morning room **(opposite)** is an essay in late nineteenth-century Chinese style, from the delicate bamboo furniture to the elegant pattern of the carpet which, although suggestive of a place of manufacture such as Beijing or Shanghai, is in fact Portuguese.

The décor of the small sitting room **(left above)** is notable for its panels of painted silk (in the Oriental style by a French painter), a superb bronze animal sculpture from China, and *tabourets* from Hong Kong. The combination of decorative elements is continued in the library **(left below)**.

The interpenetration of the house and surrounding vegetation is an essential characteristic of traditional Oriental homes; the view from the patio of a Bangkok living room is of abundant foliage, softening the harder lines of the structure. The effect of a room opening out on to a profusion of tropical foliage and decorative pots is repeated in a Western-style sitting room, from which sliding doors lead into an intimate town garden **(inset)**.

Plants, shrubs and trees in a Bangkok garden are deliberately cultivated close to the series of connected buildings which constitute the traditional home **(opposite)**. The proximity of such abundant foliage emphasizes the symbiotic relationship between man and his environment which is so integral to Thai Buddhism; amidst the profusion of vegetation, man-made objects such as statues or wooden drums **(right)** epitomize this interdependence. It is also considered fortuitous for the future prosperity and happiness of the family to encourage natural forms in and around the dwelling, as these are believed to harbour animistic spirits whose patronage and support can help the inhabitants.

The traditional Japanese garden (right and opposite) is designed and cultivated to be viewed ideally from within the house, preferably from a seated vantage point on a *tatami* mat or verandah just beyond the *shoji*. The layout is intended to provoke not only visual interest but also a profounder sense of satisfaction derived from contemplation, through a symbolic re-creation of nature in microcosm. In order to heighten the sense of limitless distance, an interesting *trompe l'oeil* technique is occasionally used in smaller gardens; large-leaved plants are placed close to the house, while smaller-leaved shrubs and bushes are located at the outer edges of the vista, thus making the boundaries seem further from us than they actually are.

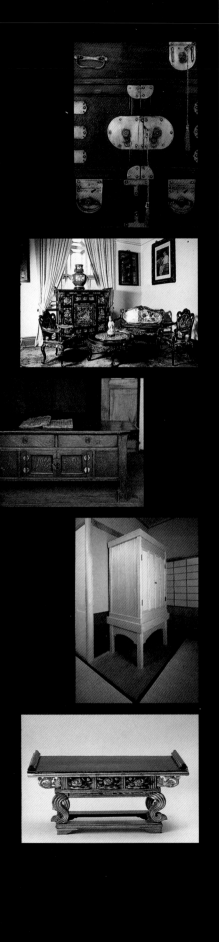

FURNITURE AND FURNISHINGS

The fascination of the Orient and recurring fashions for objects from Asia make it hardly a matter for surprise that a great deal of furniture from south-east Asia can be found in the West, like the chairs and chest in this apartment **(opposite)**. Given the relative lack of large articles in the traditional Oriental interior, much that has been made for the Western market is in fact based on pieces more commonly found in palaces or temples rather than in domestic settings. Designs, materials and decorative processes, even in contemporary furniture and furnishings, always reflect traditional attitudes and practices: high standards of craftsmanship and a genuine respect for raw materials.

The range of attractive furniture and furnishings from the East is rich indeed: lacquerwork, silks, finely-made rosewood furniture, with chests, tables and beds for every occasion. Lacquer is considered especially attractive in the West; the process, first discovered in China and then taken up in Korea and Japan, lends a great subtlety and depth of finish to the basic material, usually soft pine wood in the case of furniture, although it can be applied to fabric, bronze, porcelain and basketry. Colours range from cinnabar red, black and yellow to the crimson, vermilion and olive-green of traditional Chinese lacquer-makers. Such rich colours may not suit all tastes, but there are plenty of alternative types of furniture, such as woven cane and rattan.

Certain characteristic types of furniture have proved immensely popular in non-Oriental settings. Traditional pieces for storage – cabinets, cupboards, chests and trunks – have brought both fine finish and practicality to many a Western interior. Folding screens from the Far East were among the most avidly collected imports during the late nineteenth century and they still make an imposing addition to interiors with an Orientalist bent. Sleeping Oriental-style offers a variety of options, from the supremely practical and minimalist *futon* to the four-poster Chinese marriage bed; these latter were often made of delicately scented woods, then painted or lacquered red. Whatever your taste and purse, auctions and second-hand shops will prove fruitful locations for finding authentic Oriental-style furniture.

The traditional wooden Japanese *kaidan-dansu* storage chest fits under a staircase, providing valuable extra space. The geometric theme continues in the set of lacquered, tiered boxes from Thailand, and in the chequerboard design of a Tibetan rug.

The angles created by a Chinese screen break up the wall space and provide a perfect backdrop to the Boddhisatva statue. Similarly, a Japanese woven basket on the chest and the use of plants add texture to this rectilinear setting.

Antique Korean medicine and scholars' chests (left above and below) provide useful storage for small items, and their rich, dark wood and chased brass fittings are extremely attractive. The decorative effect in these London living rooms is heightened by the balanced arrangement of Karen hill-tribe baskets from Thailand's Golden Triangle and Chinese 'double happiness' ceramics.

The sinuous sculptural form of a Lahu hill-tribe musical instrument **(opposite)** echoes the lines of the Breuer 'Wassily' chair. The small Japanese *kuruma-dansu* (wheeled chest) contrasts with the striking sofa covers and blinds of Thai silk – the result being a successful synthesis of East and West.

The increasing availability in the West of furniture and furnishing materials from the countries of the Far East has made possible the creation of whole Oriental interior schemes, using either eclectic arrangements drawing on a variety of national styles, or furniture from a single country. From the cheapest Chinese lacquered cardboard portmanteau, to the modestly priced Korean wedding chest, to the most exquisite Japanese screen, with mother-of-pearl inlay, Oriental furniture can now be found in the West at all price levels to fulfil every function in the home. The stylized lines of Chinese altar tables **(opposite and below)** provide perfect foils to the sculptural qualities of Chinese 'scholars' rocks' and other decorative objects.

The wooden furniture of Indonesia is the result of a blend of influences, encompassing both a succession of European colonial styles and the continual, underlying reliance upon traditional zoomorphic or natural forms as stylistic motifs. Two impressive carver chairs with woven cane seats flank a table in an alcove of a London living-room **(below)**; despite their initially Western look, their Indonesian origins are revealed in the flowing, organic curves of the carcases, a theme reiterated in the anthropomorphic forms of a pair of Indonesian carvings which are used as tie-backs for the curtains, and in the use of a curvilinear animal sculpture as a focal point on the table-top.

In the same apartment (above), a weighty-looking wooden glass-fronted cabinet is used to display a collection of Oriental ceramics; the design of the chest and its decorative pediment is an unusual fusion of European Colonial and Chinese influences, but the quality of the craftsmanship and the materials used make it unmistakably Indonesian.

Much of the contemporary manufacture of wooden furniture in China is based in the areas around Jiangsu and Shanghai, using imported hardwoods from a variety of sources. A pair of restrained modern Chinese chairs in traditional style flank a highly decorative side-table in a London apartment **(opposite)**, and a matching chair and desk set in a study decorated with Oriental artefacts offers a practical and highly attractive working environment **(right)**.

Oriental screens can be successfully used in Western homes for the dual purposes for which they were originally created; firstly, they fulfil a decorative role by portraying a scene in brilliant and resonant colours, and secondly they are useful room dividers, either making the interior more intimate or simply masking an area not considered worthy of public scrutiny. Mounted on a wall and displayed flat, an antique lacquered screen has a fascinating graphic appeal and one of its panels opens to give access to a bathroom **(left above)**, while a folded four-panel painted screen breaks up an awkward corner **(left below)**. In a Western building whose aesthetic is rigorously functional, the architect has taken up the lesson of space management from the Japanese in the provision of two suspended screens to give a sense of intimacy to a seating area **(opposite)**.

The subject matter of traditional Oriental screens reflects the ideals, aspirations and values of the societies responsible for their creation; hence, natural forms such as plants and flowers and real or imaginary beasts have a symbolic significance far beyond their considerable decorative qualities **(opposite above).** Our ancestors were also fascinated by the absence of Western-style depictions of perspectival space, as portrayed in the almost axionometric cityscape on an antique eight-panelled screen **(opposite below)**. However, perhaps the most appealing facet of Chinese screens is their astonishing craftsmanship and skilful rendering of detail, such as in the two eighteenth-century carved jade table screens **(above)**.

Decorative objects from the East suitable for use in Western interiors vary from fine and rare antiques to more financially accessible objects, which may also have a strictly practical use. This selection of jars, statuary and furniture **(left and left below)** is mainly from Thailand and typifies the range of Oriental artefacts readily available at specialist shops in the West; such screens, tables and mirrors bring a decorative and exotic air to any interior. Both Oriental object and technique are present in this corner of a splendid London living room **(opposite)**; a pair of rare seventeenth-century Chinese ceramic birds adorn the top of an eighteenth-century English lacquer commode.

Ornate mirrors from the Far East make a pleasing addition to Orientalist settings. The user of the lavishly carved Burmese dressing table **(above left)** kneels on the floor to apply cosmetics; the style of this piece reveals a profound Indian influence. A large mirror in an entrance hall adds to the illusion of space **(above right)**, while the form and workmanship of an elegant Indonesian dressing table and stool in a Balinese house is a fusion of native and colonial styles **(opposite)**.

The basic carcases of many Oriental storage cabinets and chests tend to be rectangular and rather solid in form, but they often carry extremely inventive detailing and workmanship. The rich, honey-coloured *huang huali* wood of a Chinese cabinet in two sections **(above)** has been intricately carved in light-relief to depict a continuous pattern of dragons chasing pearls, while a pair of cabinets in the same material **(centre)** have open fretwork panels in a geometric design. Smaller lacquered Japanese chests feature asymmetrical designs based on natural forms **(opposite above and below)**.

The Oriental options in bedding are many; the epitome of unobtrusive simplicity and comfort is undoubtedly the Japanese *futon*, or soft cotton mattress **(far left above)**, which can be folded to make seating or stored when not required **(left above)**. Enterprising Western manufacturers are currently reworking the traditional *futon*; a rectilinear 'four-poster' *futon*, hung with swathes of draped fabric, has an understated elegance **(left below)**.

By contrast, the traditional beds of Thailand have a rather more sensuous appeal because of their carved, curvilinear forms. In an uncluttered domestic setting in Spain **(left)**, an antique Thai bedbase harmonizes with a Burmese monastery chest, while the exuberant pierced carving of a high-sided bedframe in a Bangkok emporium **(below)** evokes a rather more opulent mood.

Contemporary Philippine manufacturers produce new furniture to traditional designs; a sense of intimacy in a large room **(opposite)** is achieved by the grouping of woven cane seats around a limed teak table.

The more rugged forms of Chinese bamboo and split cane furniture are extremely sturdy and have a pleasingly tactile appearance; they are especially effective visually when placed alongside a wide variety of other Oriental pieces, such as large Chinese baskets **(left)** or a collection of Tibetan religious artefacts **(below)**.

An entirely personal Oriental style can be created by combining the objects and artefacts of a number of countries in a single interior, purely out of a sense of pleasure in the final result. These three living rooms are in London **(above left)**, Belgium **(below left)** and Spain **(opposite)**, but they share a common understanding of the Oriental appreciation of adding visually appealing elements to everyday life.

The majority of Oriental furniture to be found in the West consists of simple, generally unadorned pieces, the materials of which are untreated beyond the use of coloured stains and varnish. However, smaller pieces are frequently intricately decorated, especially in the case of screens and ornamental small chests or boxes. The stunning craftsmanship of these antique Japanese pieces **(right)** reveals a remarkable facility with lacquer and inlay; the choice of subject matter reveals the fundamental Far Eastern preoccupations with nature and trade.

DECORATIVE DETAIL

Attention to detail marks every aspect of Oriental life, from the wrapping of gifts to the presentation of food. In Far Eastern architecture, art and design, the appropriate use of the finer points of decoration and colour combination are considered to be of paramount importance. In this London apartment **(opposite)** colours and objects create an emphatically Oriental feeling.

The use of colour carries deep symbolic implications; in traditional Chinese belief the 'five colours' (blue, red, yellow, white and black) correspond to the 'five elements' (wood, fire, earth, metal and water). Red, a *yang* (male) colour, is associated with good fortune and environments where decisions must be made. Such *yin* (female) colours as green and blue are better suited to rooms given over to thought and contemplation.

The earliest Oriental artifacts to be avidly sought after in the West were ceramics from China, which make wonderfully decorative displays in any setting. Textiles, too, can be displayed on light-coloured walls to great effect. Heavily embroidered wool or silk Chinese shawls were highly fashionable in Europe and America. Deliberately produced for the West, they can still be found at auctions or in antique shops – a striking combination of traditional Oriental materials, motifs and workmanship. On the West Coast of the United States there is a vigorous trade in *nobori*, the narrow cotton banners of Japan, while displays of antique *kimonos* combine fine textiles with sculptural form.

The display of small-scale decorative artifacts grouped together is a frequent device in Oriental interiors. Prints, hangings scrolls and examples of fine calligraphy make lively but essentially uncluttered wall decorations. Miniaturization and fine detailing characterize many categories of object, from statuary to hairpins and jade carvings. Perhaps the epitome of this approach to decoration is the Japanese *netsuke*, or carved belt toggle, which was used to secure pouches through the sash of the *kimono*. These exquisite sculptures are very much sought after by collectors, but a number of Western museums now sell good-quality reproductions of these tiny, vital forms – in concept and execution the essence of Oriental decorative style.

The *cho-fa* or decorative roof finial of Thailand is used as a protective device on temple roofs and is laden with symbolic significance; its distinctive sinuous form is intended to guard against evil spirits and mishaps. Great store is placed on using precious materials for *cho-fa* and they are frequently covered with gold leaf or inlaid with precious stones **(opposite)**. These abstract sculptural forms evolved from the belief in the protective powers of the *naga* or mythical water serpent of Thailand **(opposite right above and below, above and above right)**; when they have outlived their usefulness, the *cho-fa* may make a fascinating sculptural addition to an Oriental-style interior **(right below)**.

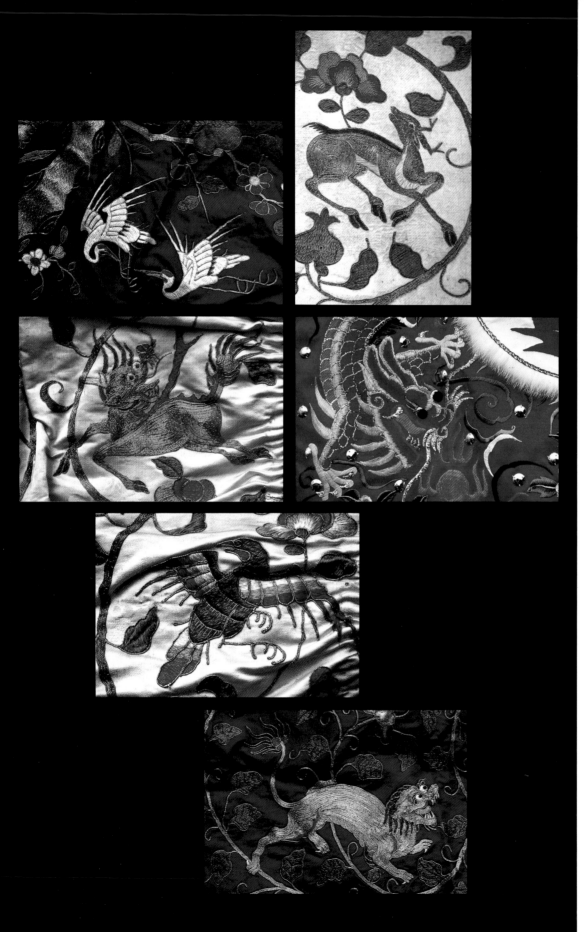

Interesting combinations of colour and motif are not necessarily confined to the finest of Oriental textiles. The traditional Thai silk embroidery **(left)** is clearly of high and enduring quality, but this display in a London emporium of decorative cushions **(opposite)** from all over the Far East shows a source of decorative delight at very modest cost.

A selection of bamboo wedding baskets and details from mainland China **(opposite)**. Traditionally, young couples would receive wedding presents in these containers. The three tiers separate, providing a compact and portable method of storing numerous household items. They make striking free-standing ornaments, either placed on the floor or on a large article of furniture, such as a chest.

The careful selection of a few Oriental artefacts adds visual impact and drama to a Western interior **(right)**. An antique Japanese *tansu*, a painted Chinese wedding basket and a colourful Tibetan mask of papier-mâché provide vivid contrasts to the cool, rectilinear simplicity of this hallway.

The startling variety of shapes and forms to be found in traditional Thai and Burmese lacquer bowls and food stands is a manifestation of the Oriental desire to act appropriately on particular occasions. Families consider it important to show respect and hospitality to their visitors by serving food in the correct and most attractive container **(opposite)**. The resonant colour of an antique Burmese lacquer food bowl glows from its monochromatic setting, and its simple form sits perfectly on an overtly Modernist table by Eileen Gray **(left)**.

The use of ornate Japanese lacquerware in an otherwise minimalist Western setting introduces resonant, vibrant colour and fascinating detail. The fan-shaped stacking box, nesting trays and armrest are shown to their best advantage combined on a low table in the drawing room **(right)**.

The low-level viewpoint and the uncluttered simplicity of the hallway **(opposite)** is heightened by the careful positioning of three exquisitely lacquered retinue trunks below framed *ukiyo-e* woodblock prints, while the solid carcase of the chest provides a perfect plinth for the bizarre forms of a *bonsai* miniature tree.

Collecting and displaying Oriental objects together can be visually satisfying and add to the character of a room. The smooth, rounded forms and the rich colours of a variety of red and black lacquer bowls from Thailand and Burma are shown to their best advantage housed in alcove shelving around a Spanish fireplace **(left)**.

A Japanese *kaidan-dansu* or staircase chest (above left) provides a fascinating stepped display case for pieces of Indonesian ivory and Ban Prasat Thai pots. Antique blue and white Chinese porcelain sits well on contemporary shelving **(above right)**.

Old Oriental pieces surprise and intrigue
the viewer when placed in a contemporary Western
setting. A wooden figure of the Buddha sits serenely
in a stairwell **(above)**, while a Japanese *hibachi*, or
brazier, provides a home for houseplants
(opposite).

Predominantly monochromatic settings allow the colours
and textures of Oriental pieces to become fascinating focal points. A
collection of Japanese lacquered miniature furniture sits jewel-like on
a glass table **(above left)**; the rugged simplicity of two Tibetan
trunks adds weight and solidity to a hallway **(above right)**, while a
Spanish open-plan drawing room houses modern Philippino cane
furniture and an angle of the stairs houses a woven basket from the
Karen hill-tribes of Thailand **(opposite)**.

Oriental statuary has a particularly evocative power and can be used to create or define the atmosphere of a room. An uplit Khmer mask **(left)** has a surreal, disembodied quality, while the antique stone Buddha simply placed as a central piece in a living room provides an atmosphere of calm and tranquility **(opposite)**.

A French apartment which uses Oriental figures and artefacts as focal points; hanging bamboo blinds cover the windows and divide the drawing room, while allowing light to filter through; an altar table supports a pair of red Chinese vases and a seventeenth-century *cloisonné* bowl from the Imperial Palace **(left above)**. Large scale sculptural pieces dominate this interior, including a rare antique Buddhist statue, carved wooden buffalo from Indonesia **(left below)** and a mounted *cho-fa* or Thai temple roof finial **(opposite)**.

The intricacy of form and the delicacy of decorative detail of eighteenth-century chinoiserie is recalled in a Western setting; ceramic Chinese *fo* dogs guard the bedchamber **(left)**, Indonesian animals settle on a table **(below)** while a precocity of carving of stylized clouds decorates a Chinese table **(opposite)**, below which is the reclining figure of an eighteenth-century Burmese Buddha.

Rugs and textiles are among the most easily transportable and durable of all decorative artefacts from the Far East. Their stylized motifs and vibrant colours add an authentic Oriental atmosphere to Western interiors, as in this London house **(below)**. This room is dominated by a tiger rug from Tibet; these are especially popular in the West for their rich imagery and traditional associations. Indonesian rugs make an important contribution to the sense of luxury and exuberance in this London apartment **(opposite)**.

Decorative details can also play a vital part in creating an Oriental-style garden; Thai craftsmen are extremely adept at creating reproduction 'antique' statues, such as a mythical Khmer figure **(above left)**, while the fo dog or guardian lion is becoming increasingly available in the West, as modern Chinese marble statues in traditional forms are currently manufactured in Tianjin and are available in many major Western cities **(above centre)**. Ceramic vessels and wooden mill cogs provoke curiosity, especially when partially concealed by verdant undergrowth **(above right and opposite)**.

Auction houses and the showrooms and galleries of specialists and dealers are fascinating places to visit, and a rich source of both goods and inspiration for the would-be Oriental stylist.

Acknowledgments

The authors and publishers wish to extend especial thanks to the people and organizations below for their substantial help and guidance in the creation of this book.

Percy Barkes and Delia Su, Charlotte Barnes, Beagle Gallery, Jean-Michel Beurdeley, Michael Birch, Yui Ying Brown, The Buddhist Centre, Carroll, Dempsey & Thirkell, Odile Cavendish, Margaret Caselton, David Chipperfield Associates, Peter Cook, Shirley Day, Michael Dean, Walter Donahue, Kevin Donnelly, Françoise Durand of Agence Top, Fine Art Photographs, Sheila Fitzjones, Gerda Flockinger, Jonathan Gale, Caroline Gearey of the Bridgeman Art Library, Felicity Golden, Stephen Greenberg and Dean Hawkes, Khum Fa Ham, Lillian Hochhauser, Hong Kong Tourism Authority, Takashi Inaba, Japan National Tourist Organisation, Lena and Talal Kanafani, Korean National Tourist Corporation, The Lacquer Factory, Saigon, C. T. Loo et Cie, Hansjorg Mayer, Hidetoshi Mujagi, Klaus Müller, Sylvia Napier, Neal Street East, Ambassadress Josephine de Oliveira Maia, Old Chiangmai Cultural Centre, Rama Antiques, Ruth Orbach, Tjokorda Patra, Miranda Rothschild, The Saigon Tourist Office, David Salmon, The Siam Society of Bangkok, Paul Sibbering, Mark Slattery, Charlie Smith of Remote Treasures, Sotheby's Chinese Department, Geneviève de Taragon of Edimedia, Jim Thomson, Bill Tingey, Anongnart Ulapathorn, The Urasenke Foundation, Steve Vidler, Dieter and Susie von Boehm-Bering, Daniel and Thomas White, Henry Woods-Wilson. The apartment illustrated on p. 45 was designed by Daigre et Rybar.

Picture Credits

All the photographs in this book are the work of Michael Freeman, except the following:
p. 4 Thames & Hudson; p. 5 Futon Company (top left), Japan National Tourist Organisation (centre left), Agence Top (photo Pascal Hinous) (centre right); pp. 6, 7 Peter Cook; p. 9 Michael Jenner (a.), Sotheby's (b.); p. 10 Sotheby's; p. 11 Fine Art Photographic Library (a.l. and b.), Siân Evans (a.r.); p. 12 Luca Tettoni (a.); p. 13 Luca Tettoni; p. 22 Luca Tettoni; p. 25 Luca Tettoni (b.r.); p. 28 Luca Tettoni (a.), Bill Tingey (b.), Siân Evans (second from top); pp. 40, 41 Bill Tingey; p. 44 Hong Kong Tourism Authority (a.), Bill Tingey (second from top), Futon Co. (b.); p. 45 Agence Top (photo Pascal Hinous); pp. 64, 65, 66, 67 Keyphotos (photo Kikutani); p. 70 Agence Top (photo Pascal Hinous); p. 76 Agence Top (photo Pascal Hinous); pp. 82, 83 Keyphotos (photo Kikutani); p. 84 Hong Kong Tourism Authority (second from top), Mimi Lipton (b.); p. 96 Edimedia (photo R. Guillemot) (a.), Edimedia (photo J. Guillot) (b.); pp. 98, 99 Bridgeman Art Library; p. 100 Sheila Fitzjones; p. 101 Michael Boys; p. 104 Sotheby's; p. 105 Bridgeman Art Library (a.r. and b.r.); p. 106 Futon Co.; p. 110 Agence Top (photo Pascal Hinous) (b.); p. 114 Agence Top (photo Pascal Hinous) (second from top); p. 132, 133 Agence Top (photo Pascal Hinous); p. 134 Edimedia (photo R. Guillemot); p. 135 Edimedia (photo R. Guillemot); pp. 136, 137 Edimedia (photo R. Guillemot). All photographs on the cover are by Michael Freeman.

The photograph on p. 8 © Her Majesty Queen Elizabeth II is reproduced by gracious permission of Her Majesty Queen Elizabeth II (photo Michael Freeman).

Select Bibliography

Allane, Lee, *Chinese Rugs*, London, 1993
Allen, Jeanne, *The Designer's Guide to Japanese Patterns 3*, London, 1989
Allen, Jeanne, *The Designer's Guide to Samurai Patterns*, London, 1991
Bürer, Catherine, *Kirei: Posters from Japan 1978–1993*, London, 1994
Conner, Patrick, *Oriental Architecture in the West*, London, 1979
Dinkel, John, *The Royal Pavilion, Brighton*, London, 1983
Engel, Heino, *Measure and Construction of the Japanese House*, Vermont and Tokyo, 1985
Gillow, John, *Traditional Indonesian Textiles*, London, 1995
Hibi, Sadao, *Japanese Detail* (3 vols.), San Francisco and London, 1989
Inoue, Mitsuo, *Space in Japanese Architecture*, Tokyo and New York, 1985
Japan Art and Culture Association, *Charles Rennie Mackintosh*, Tokyo, 1985
Kaufmann, Edgar and Ben Raeburn, *Frank Lloyd Wright: Writings and Buildings*, New York, 1960
Kim, H. Edward, *The Korean Smile*, Seoul, 1983
Lee, Sherman E., *A History of Far Eastern Art*, London, 1975
Lee, Sherman E., *Japanese Decorative Style*, New York, 1972
Lip, Dr. Evelyn, *Feng Shui for the Home*, New York, 1985
Lipton, Mimi, *The Tiger Rugs of Tibet*, London, 1988
Minick, Scott and Jiao Ping, *Chinese Graphic Design in the 20th Century*, London, 1990
Powell, Andrew, *Living Buddhism*, London, 1989
Powell, Robert, *The Tropical Asian House*, London, 1996
Slesin, Suzanne, Stafford Cliff and Daniel Rozensztroch, *Japanese Style*, New York and London, 1987
Walker, Barbara and Rio Helmi, *Bali Style*, London, 1995
Warren, William and Luca Tettoni, *Arts and Crafts of Thailand*, London, 1995
Warren, William and Luca Tettoni, *Balinese Gardens*, London, 1995
Warren, William and Luca Tettoni, *Living in Thailand*, London, 1989
Watson, William, *Tang and Liao Ceramics*, London, 1984
Wichmann, Siegfried, *Japonisme*, London, 1981
Wright, Susan M., *The Decorative Arts in the Victorian Period*, London, 1989

Index